BECAUSE WE LOVE YOU
MARCUS DEAN

BECAUSE WE LOVE YOU MARCUS DEAN

This book is dedicated to my family and friends, whose unwavering support and love have always been a constant in my life.

Sometimes, parents say "No," and you might wonder why. But every "No" and every rule comes from love that reaches the sky.

When we say, "Hold my hand when we cross the street," it's not to slow you down; it's to keep you safe from speedy cars zooming through town.

When we say, "Eat your veggies and finish your fruit," it's not to be bossy; it's to help you grow big and strong, from your head to your boot!

When we say, "Wear your helmet before you ride," it's not to take extra time; it's to protect your wonderful brain inside!

When we say, "Bedtime now, no more delay," it's not to stop your fun, it's to give you energy for a bright new day!

When we say, "Look both ways before you go," it's not because we worry too much; it's to help you see what you need to know.

When we say, "Brush your teeth, morning and night," it's not just a habit—it keeps your smile sparkling and bright!

When we say, "Wash your hands after you play," it's not to make you wait; it's to keep germs far, far away.

When we say, "Tell the truth, always be kind," it's not just words we say; it helps you have friends that truly shine.

When we say, "We love you, always and true," it's because everything we do is to take care of you!

When we say it's time for school,
It's not because we're being cruel.
We love you so and want you to grow
To learn, make friends, and let your light show!

When we say "we love you," it's truly true
You're the sunshine that brightens all we do!

When we ask you to clean and put things away,
It's not to take your fun away.
We're helping you learn to care and be neat
Because a tidy space is really sweet!

When we say "be patient" or "take your turn"
It's part of the way that you learn.
To grow with kindness, heart, and grace
Because we love your smiling face!

So if we ever make a rule that you don't understand, remember, it's because we love you, and we're always holding your hand.